the
poems of

Nakahara
Chūya

中原中也詩集

the
poems of

Nakahara Chūya

translated by Paul Mackintosh
and Maki Sugiyama

First published in 1993, reprinted 2017

Gracewing
2 Southern Avenue
Leominster
Herefordshire HR6 0QF

www.gracewing.co.uk

© 1993, 2017 Gracewing Publishing

© 1993 Translation by Paul Mackintosh and Maki Sugiyama

ISBN 978 0 85244 255 5

Cover design by Gill Onions

Calligraphy by Maki Sugiyama

Typesetting by The Choir Press, Gloucester

Contents

Introduction

Nakahara Chūya (1907–37) received little recognition during his lifetime. His verse, deemed obscure, was little read; he compiled only two collections and published only one before his early death. However, amongst his devoted admirers were some of the most talented and influential writers and critics of his generation, and since 1945 his work has risen from relative obscurity to occupy a central place in the canon of Japanese modernism. His dissolute, bohemian existence in Tokyo, his complicated love-life and his early death have all fostered the image of a *poète maudit*, hounded through his short life by a vengeful fate. Many reminiscences of Nakahara have been published, some by his own family, and the secondary literature is now extensive. His poems are treasured for their straightforward colloquialism, their resonant simplicity and their unique rhythm of languor, sorrow and sentiment.

Nakahara Chūya was born on 29 April 1907, the first child of a family which later numbered six sons. His birthplace, Yuda (now part of Yamaguchi City), was in Yamaguchi Prefecture on the far western tip of Honshu – the Japanese 'mainland' – next to the island of Kyushu. His father, Nakahara Kensuke, was a military doctor, serving in Korea at the time of his son's birth. A man of some literary pretensions, he had contributed stories to the newspapers with the aim of following in the giant footsteps of Mori Ōgai, who had risen to the rank of Surgeon General of the army medical ·corps whilst revolutionizing Japanese literature. Nakahara's mother, Fuku, had lost her father while she was young and had subsequently been adopted by her uncle. Nakahara's foster-grandparents were Catholics, and early on they introduced him to the faith. Yamaguchi was a centre of the Christianity which had been introduced into western Japan in the sixteenth century, and Nakahara's later religious attitudes were nurtured in this environment.

Nakahara was spoiled as a child, even by the standards of a Japanese first son. His parents forbade him to swim in the river with his brothers, or to play with other local children; to chastise him, his father would strike him with a handkerchief. As the child of fairly wealthy upper-middle-class parents, he never suffered material want, and he often relied on the generosity of his family in later life. Subsequently he complained of the odd mixture of rigour and indulgence that marked, and marred, his upbringing; but there is no doubt that he was a contented child, and that the happiness of this time contributed to the personal myth of infantine bliss which he would articulate so eloquently later on.

When Nakahara was eight years old, his brother Tsugurō, nicknamed Arō, died of meningitis. He wrote a poem grieving over the death, which he later recorded as the first stirring of his poetic impulse: 'on a really cold morning, I wrote a poem about my brother, who died in the New Year of that year, and that was the first time' (*Poetic CV*, 1936). Nakahara was a gifted child − even dubbed a prodigy. At the age of eleven, he began writing tanka regularly, and contributed them to the local newspaper *Bōchō-Shinbun* and the magazine *Fujingahō*. This early involvement with the classical form of the tanka is reflected in his mature poems, many of which were written in the traditional 5-7 syllable metre.

In 1920 Nakahara passed the entrance examination for the Yamaguchi Chūgaku (middle school) with excellent grades. Whilst at the school, he issued a collection of tanka called *Sugurono* with his friends; but in March 1923 he failed his third year examination, having devoted too much time to literature. It was a great humiliation for both the erstwhile prodigy and his family, and Nakahara was sent to the private Ritsumeikan middle school in Kyoto to make up lost ground. 'I felt like flying away, leaving my parents for the first time'

ix

(*Poetic CV*). He no longer wrote tanka, but began to compose poems in a looser, more modern style. He read *The Divine Comedy* in translation; and in the autumn of 1923 he came across a copy of the *Poems of Dadaist Shinkichi* in a second-hand bookshop. This early example of Japanese Dada inspired Nakahara, who henceforth incorporated outré imagery and often obscure sound-symbolism into his work.

According to his *Poetic CV*, 'from 1923 to October 1933 I went for a walk every day. I would read through the night, sleep in the morning and get up at noon, then go for a walk until midnight.' The things that he saw on his daily walk, and the conversations he had with his friends, became the materials for his poems.

By April 1924 the precocious teenager was living with an aspiring actress, Hasegawa Yasuko, three years older than himself. A famous photograph taken at about this time shows a boy with large soulful eyes, full lips and a small, firm chin, who wore his straight hair long and affected a big dark hat. That autumn, he met through one of his teachers the poet Tominaga Tarō (1901–25), who introduced him to the works of Baudelaire, Rimbaud and Verlaine. The example of French Symbolist poetry, at first in translation and later in the original, was to be another formative influence on Nakahara, who began to produce verse of extreme musicality *à la* Verlaine, featuring Symbolist staples such as pierrots.

Tominaga's example prompted Nakahara to leave school in March 1925 without receiving his final certificate and move to Tokyo along with Yasuko, who cherished dreams of film stardom. The world of Japanese poetry that Nakahara entered was dominated by the new genre of 'shi' poetry, employing free-style verse and colloquial language, which had appeared in the Taishō era (1912–26). The traditional forms that had been current in the Meiji era (1868–1912), though still practised and often the vehicles for challenging modern writing, had yielded prominence to more Westernized poems of romantic love or realism. Two dominant streams of thought and practice characterized the 1910s and early 20s: the humanist aestheticism of the magazine *Kanjō* (Feelings), founded in 1916 by Murō Saisei and Hagiwara Sakutarō and more or less allied to the Shirakaba (White Birch) coterie of writers; and the more socialist Minshūshi (People's Poetry) group, formed in 1918. Artistically, the former was the more influential. Murō's first collection *Ai no Shishū* (Poems of Love) gained immediate popularity and became a modern classic, whilst Hagiwara's collection *Tsuki ni Hoeru* (Howling at the Moon, 1917) was even more successful in establishing the possibility of a fully modern, native poetic sensibility.

European developments led to the introduction of Futurism and Dada into Japan, in the shape of Takahashi Shinkichi's 'Dadaist Manifesto' and the magazines *Aka to Kuro* (1922–4) and *A* (1924–8). *A* was the immediate forerunner of *Shi to Shiron* (Poetry and Poetics), which ran from September 1928 to December 1931, a central organ of modern poetry and theory characteristic of the beginning of the Shōwa era (1926–89). *Shi to Shiron*'s pure poetry was opposed by a proletarian literature movement and more than 10 left-wing coterie magazines – none of which achieved any enduring reputation. Only one other magazine of the time is still highly valued: *Dora* (Gong) founded in 1925 by Kusano Shinpei and numbering contributors such as Miyazawa Kenji and Takamura Kōtarō. *Dora* became *Rekitei* (The Course of History) in 1935. Nakahara was a regular contributor.

Despite Nakahara's early interest in Dada, he had nothing to do with the left-wing stance of the Dadaist magazines, following his own individual aesthetic bent. After his arrival he became acquainted through Tominaga with Kobayashi Hideo (1902–83), at that time still a student at the élite Tokyo University, but soon to make his mark as Japan's leading literary critic and an original thinker who was, according to the eminent Japanologist Edward Seidensticker, 'a better writer than most of the novelists who have occupied the translators.' Kobayashi, who wrote his 1928 graduation thesis on Rimbaud, was clearly congenial company for Nakahara; furthermore, his circle included Kawakami Tetsutarō (1902–80), later a prominent critic, and the future novelist Ōoka Shōhei (1909 – 88).

Nakahara later declared that in August 1925, 'I more or less decided to devote myself to poetry' (*Poetic CV*). But in November Yasuko left Nakahara for Kobayashi. The incident was a turning point in Nakahara's life: more than the end of a first love, it marked a catastrophic loss of innocence, and Nakahara alluded to the pain of that loss constantly throughout the rest of his life. After his death, an essay on the incident was found, entitled 'My Life': '...I was utterly mortified...because of the incident, I lost the onetime peace of self-coherence.' Virtually all his work of enduring value dates from after November 1925. But, for the time being, the result was 'a peculiar love triangle based on mutual co-operation.' Nakahara called on Kobayashi and Yasuko regularly, until the couple finally fled to Kamakura to escape his attentions.

Nakahara led a wayward lifestyle, supported by money from his ever-indulgent parents. Once he had made a new acquaintance, he would move in nearby and visit that friend all the time. However, his comrades soon lost patience with his contrariness, egoism, and peculiar Dadaistic behaviour, and quickly became estranged. When alone with a companion, he was charming, but in groups of three or more he became strident and overbearing. A heavy drinker, he would often provoke fights, but as he was small and lightly built he usually fared worst.

In 1926 Nakahara wrote 'Morning Song': 'my policy was more or less fixed by 'Morning Song'; however, I was disappointed that it required so much effort to write a poem of only fourteen lines' (*Poetic CV*). This is generally regarded as his first substantial poem. The fourteen-line pseudo-sonnet was a popular format at the time amongst the 'shi' poets. The use of 5-7 syllable metre, the traditional Japanese ballad metre, was also fairly customary at the time; it contributed the songlike quality to this and so many of Nakahara's subsequent poems. The tone of wistful regret, the surreal juxtaposition of impressions, are already the true note of Nakahara:

along the embankment,   melting away...
the beautiful,   various dreams.

Understanding how and why Nakahara imports a resinous
odour into the poem and links light coming through his door
with the sound of a military band would perhaps enable
complete comprehension of the piece; but the important
thing, as with much of Nakahara's work, is the pure
registration of the moment and mood. Nakahara was often
prone to insert and link recondite images or even meaningless
sounds in his verse without explanation, almost always with
the clear intention of chiming in an emotional or aesthetic
association, like a chord in music.

Nakahara did not, apparently, regard the extreme
subjectivity of his verse as a limitation. In a letter to
Kawakami Tetsutarō (1927–8), he declared 'I deal with
nature, but artificially. Subjectivity comes first. Then the
symbol has its place. Then it's not mimesis, but song.'

Kawakami, who first met Nakahara in 1927, left a vivid
record of his impressions at this time: 'Nakahara was walking
with his hands in his jacket pockets, in an outfit exactly like
Rimbaud's in the portrait that Verlaine drew: black clothes
and shirt, and a broad-brimmed hat, with hair hanging over
the neck. His behaviour was extraordinary. I listened to him,
feeling a strange mixture of curiosity, fascination and disgust'
(*Shiki*, Nakahara Chūya memorial issue).

Kawakami introduced Nakahara to the composer Moroi
Saburō and the music group Suruya. Tokyo intellectuals of
this time shared a general enthusiasm for Western music:
Kobayashi himself could play both violin and mandolin.
Nakahara himself developed a wide-ranging interest in music.
In May 1928, his 'Morning Song' and 'The Hour of Death'
were sung in a Suruya concert, to settings by Moroi.
'Homecoming', 'Spring and the Baby' and 'Lost Hope' were
also set to music: Nakahara is thought to have written the
latter specifically as a song lyric. The proliferation of radio
gradually infiltrated Nakahara's songs, which were relatively
easy to follow and appreciate, into public awareness. Also in

xiii

May, Kobayashi terminated his stormy relationship with Yasuko. Nakahara tried to win her back, but was rebuffed. His father died that same year.

In April 1929 a coterie magazine, *Hakuchigun*, was founded. The name, chosen by Nakahara, meant a gathering of fools incapable of mustering any ambition even if they wished to; other members of the coterie included his friends Kawakami Tetsutarō, Ōoka Shōhei, and the critic Abe Rokurō (1904–57). Nakahara contributed energetically to *Hakuchigun* until it ceased publication the following year after its sixth issue. One night in June that year, drunk as so often before, Nakahara smashed a doorlight – unfortunately, he had chosen a ward assemblyman's house. He was locked up in a detention cell for two weeks, and developed a chronic fear of the police.

In 1930 Nakahara entered a tutorial college to train as a diplomatic secretary; a first step towards going to France. However, after he finished the course a couple of years later he gave up the plan. He wrote to his friend Yasuhara, 'by all means I want to go to Paris, either in the spring or the autumn. I would go if only I could forget about Yasuko.' In December 1930, Yasuko, who had been keeping other company since her breakup with Kobayashi, gave birth to an illegitimate child. Nakahara acted as a godfather to the child, and lavished affection on him as if he were his own son. (Yasuko later married a businessman.) Another of his brothers, Kōzō, died in 1931.

In 1931 the proletarian literature movement was forced to dissolve, amidst coerced recantations, by government pressure following the Manchurian Incident. *Shi to Shiron* ceased publication in 1931 as major contributors such as Kitagawa Fuyuhiko and Miyoshi Tatsuji departed for the new *Shi, Genjitsu* (Poetry and Reality). *Shi, Genjitsu* continued for about a year from 1930, and a similar magazine, *Jikan* (Time), appeared about the same time. These two merged in 1933 to become *Shiki* (Four Seasons), as part of a politically conservative reaction against the extreme intellectualism and modernism of *Shi to Shiron*, which favoured a more lyric poetry. Many of Nakahara's later appearances were in the pages of *Shiki*. Kobayashi founded the magazine *Bungakukai* (Literary World) with Kawabata Yasunari and others in 1933, becoming its editor in June 1935; and his presence ensured that Nakahara received favourable mention there.

In April 1932 Nakahara began editing his first collection, *Yagi no Uta* (Goat Songs). The title was presumably conceived because Nakahara was born in the Year of the Sheep and, thanks to his small chin and protruding ears, felt some affinity to goats and sheep. No publisher rated the work highly enough to support an edition, so he began thinking of private publication. In June a notice for subscription was issued, but only ten of the proposed 200 copies were subscribed for. The notice was issued again in July, with identical results. Nakahara's literary friends refused to subscribe because they feared he would squander the subscription fees on drink. Printing finally began in September, paid for by donations from Nakahara's mother, but ceased when these funds ran out. The collection eventually appeared in December 1934.

Yagi no Uta contained 44 poems, written between 1924 and 1930, ten of which had appeared in various magazines. Inevitably, the material was diverse and uneven, but it established Nakahara's poetic voice and includes some of his best, most characteristic work.

At the time, the closest to a poetic mainstream was a modernist-oriented aesthetic, typified by *Shi to Shiron*, which took little account of the ostensible content of verse. That magazine's editors contended that what mattered in poesy was the way in which it was written, and that the meaning of the words written belonged to the separate domain of literature. Nakahara's stance in respect to prevailing critical opinion was therefore anomalous, since his work constantly laid stress on meaning. However, Kobayashi praised Nakahara highly in *Bungakukai* soon after the publication of *Yagi no Uta*. 'His poems are admirable, or rather his poetic mind is admirable. It is most difficult to keep a purely poetic mind without absconding from the sense of the times, in a time of confusion of tongues like today. Nakahara is a poet who is doing so, and he is doing so because he was born with a nature such that he cannot live without doing so, rather than making efforts to do so. I think this is an unusual configuration...Nakahara's poems are unusual in respect of expressing wounded lyric spirit with bold frankness...[then Kobayashi quotes 'Soiled Sorrow'] Nakahara's poems are always chanted from some place like this. He never escapes into either intellect, or mentality, or sensation. The anguish of his nature by which he can't escape becomes poetry itself.' Nakahara himself said, 'People's first reflection is to blame for first making them unhappy. That first reflection made people political. In any case, even if reflection is to blame, we became political animals. I am, after all, a lamenter who never regrets the fact of having become one.' He quoted this opening to his 1926 'Poetic Manifesto' in his *Poetic CV* of 1936.

Nakahara loathed politics and society. He never had a job in his life. He grieves in 'Dusk' and repines over his character as a political animal in 'Soiled Sorrow'. And he criticizes his parents, who raised him strictly to make him so, in 'Miscreant's Song'. In 'Memorandum on Art', he wrote '"This is a hand", the hand you feel before saying the word "hand"; it is good so long as you feel that hand deeply...Art is work in the world before the word.' And this is Nakahara's basic idea. A similar expression can be seen in 'The Voice of Life's last sentence. 'The world before the word' is the opposite of the hated 'politics' and embodies the supreme bliss of his childhood. Nakahara recalls this childhood bliss in 'Morning Song', and 'Shambolic Town Elegy', another record of his 'past days'.

The language of the poems varies between literary diction and the modern colloquial. Both registers were lucid and easy to follow; more idiosyncratic was the sound symbolism of some poems. In 'Circus', for instance, the famous refrain –

yu-an, yu-yon, yu-ya-yu-yon

– repeated several times throughout the poem is without apparent meaning. Japanese employs onomatopoeia more than do any of the European languages, but this line is Nakahara's own coinage. It could be taken to refer to the swinging trapeze artist in the circus, but essentially the reader can make what he will of it. It does, however, contribute to the musicality of the verse; and Nakahara emphasized the music of other poems in the collection by the repetition of refrains or even whole verses, in a manner derived from Verlaine. 'Hangover' is only twelve lines long, yet the third of its three verses is a straight repetition of the first. Nakahara was effusively grateful for this lesson from European verse (which he termed 'the poem', as distinct from traditional Japanese forms): 'Its most important difference from *waka* and *haiku*, though it is a difference of degree, is that the poem, almost to a qualitative extent, has extra room for repetition, as well as the likes of acrostics and refrain' (*Poetry and Its Tradition*, 1934).

In December 1933 Nakahara married Ueno Takako, a distant relative. In the same month, his volume of translations, *Rimbaud: Poems of his School Days* was published. Ōoka Shōhei later wrote of these translations, 'Nakahara's translation may suffer some handicaps linguistically, but it is unparalleled where he captures the unity of the poetry as a whole. What's more, he translates with care regarding the gaps in the vocabulary caused by Rimbaud's haste. I would say this is most dramatic translation.' Nakahara also contributed to various literary journals including *Shiki* and *Kigen* some of the poems which were later assembled in his second collection, *Arishi Hi no Uta* (Songs of Past Days). In October 1934, his first son, Fumiya, was born. Despite his bohemian tendencies, Nakahara was devoted to his firstborn – as he was to all children, whom he regarded as embodiments of prelapsarian innocence. In 1935 he became a member of the literary coterie Rekitei, and would give readings at its meetings. 'His readings lived up to what people call "original"...his character and his poems and his reading were inseparable' (Kusano Shinpei,

Bungakukai, Nakahara memorial issue).

In June 1936 a second volume of translations, *Selected Poems of Rimbaud*, was published. But in November of that year Fumiya died of tubercular meningitis. Nakahara was shattered and suffered a nervous breakdown. The birth of his second son, Yoshimasa, in December did nothing to mitigate his grief. In January 1937 he was incarcerated in the Chiba Temple sanatorium. While in hospital, he wrote a record of his treatment, poems, tanka, essays and letters. He quickly rallied, and was released in mid-February. Unable to live in the same house with his memories of Fumiya, he decamped with his wife and child to Kamakura, where Kobayashi and Ōoka were living. That same month, his *Collection of Poems of Rimbaud* was published; he received 50 copies, in lieu of payment, which he gave away to family and friends.

In September, fatigued both mentally and physically, he decided to return to Yamaguchi. 'I feel I am running on like a mechanical doll. When I can't really help myself, I drink beer even in the morning or noon. I can manage for the time being with two small bottles...there would not be anything nice if I go back, but I feel some adherence somehow as my childhood clings to even a little street corner' (letter addressed to Yasuhara, dated 2 September). He began to suffer from chronic appetite dysfunction, especially a tendency to eat until bloated, possibly a symptom of slight brain damage due to tubercular infection. He finished editing *Arishi Hi no Uta* and entrusted Kobayashi with the manuscript. In the postscript he had prepared for the volume, he wrote, 'Now I put the manuscripts together and entrust them to my friend Kobayashi Hideo, then retire to my hometown, leaving Tokyo after these thirteen years. I do not have any particular plans but I think I am going to be engrossed in poetry at last. Well, what will happen after that...when I think about it, I don't have the faintest idea. Farewell Tokyo! Oh, my youth!'

On 5 October Nakahara fell ill and was hospitalized. Yasuko and her new husband paid him a visit on 21 October, but by that time he was delirious. After a final brief return to lucidity, he died on 22 October 1937 of tubercular meningitis. His second son died in January 1938.

Kobayashi commented on Nakahara's remaining poems in the Nakahara memorial issue of *Bungakukai*: 'Nakahara's posthumous manuscripts are gathered in a mess at my place. In fact, these are the manuscripts which Nakahara gave up working on. Therefore, apart from the poems in *Arishi Hi* which Nakahara himself selected, he admitted that they are not worth being published...If he had had a little longer before falling ill, I think he might have burnt them all.'

Arishi Hi no Uta (Songs of Past Days) contained 58 poems, most of which were written between 1925 and 1937. The volume carried a dedication: 'Dedicated to the soul of my late son Fumiya.' Nakahara wrote in his diary in July 1936, 'Bequeathed item – I hope Fumiya will like poetry. I believe we could do pretty much in two generations.' Despite the oddity of a 29-year-old's talk of bequests, this shows how much hope Nakahara reposed in Fumiya. 'Song Without Words', 'Spring Evening's Reflection' and 'Feeling for a Dragonfly' express such hopes. A dead child frequently appears in Nakahara's poems – 'Moonlight', 'Shame', 'Autumn Day's Frenzy' – and in these cases the symbol also represents 'past days' and childhood bliss. Retrospection also appears in 'A Fairy Tale', 'Chōmon Gorge, Winter' and the uncollected poem 'Cicadas', specifically concerning his home. In 'Cicadas' and 'Winter Day's Remembrance' he recalled his dead brothers. Nakahara held that the deceased are pure, and that those who live on are corrupted – as recounted in 'Spring Day's Caprice'.

This touches on one important element of his verse; his sincere religious impulses. Though they seldom rise to the surface of his expression, Nakahara held clear religious convictions, usually implicit in his wide-eyed registration of things seen or felt. Writing *c*.1936, he declared 'If my intuition says that God exists, then why does it say so? Since my intuition, i.e. myself, living in this world, feels a mystery in all material phenomena, then the mystery is a joy of the soul' (*My View of Poetry*). The 'God' in question was evidently the Christian God whose creed he associated with his foster-grandparents and childhood. Friends testified to Nakahara's honest regard for Catholicism, and although he cannot be represented as a Catholic or a Christian poet, Christianity cleared helped awaken his perception of the numinous in things.

In other poems Nakahara specifically recalls his dead son. In 'Spring Will Come Again' he remembers him sadly, and in 'Spring Day's Caprice' bereavement induces 'a sense of service' obliging him to live 'not too happy and not too sad'…'at the correct tempo'. He wrote 'Moonlight' and 'Frogs' Voices' in the year of his death.

The quality of the verse in *Arishi Hi no Uta* was if anything an improvement on *Yagi no Uta*; the standard was more uniform and evenly maintained. There were fewer of the tricks and obscurities of the earlier collection; metaphor and image were more maturely and fully developed. And a new mode had entered his repertoire: a controlled clarity shown to best advantage in poems like 'Chōmon Gorge, Winter', where the recording of the scene, the expression of the sentiment, and the lyricism of the verse come together in perfect unity. Clearly, Nakahara had won his full self-confidence as an artist – a fact which makes his premature death all the more tragic.

Nakahara was buried in the family grave in his home town. A stone memorial, inscribed with lines from 'Homecoming', now stands there near his father's old clinic. After his death, both *Bungakukai* and *Shiki* published memorial issues. *Arishi Hi no Uta* appeared in April 1938: 500 copies were printed, followed by another 500 in June. But Nakahara's rise to general esteem really only began after the Second World War. *Poems of Nakahara Chūya*, published in 1947, sold almost 20,000 copies. Researchers unearthed, and continue to unearth, uncollected poems from various journals and manuscripts. Kobayashi's strictures on the drafts in his possession apply also to these, but some, such as 'Fig Leaves' and 'Slaughterhouse', are now regarded as comparable to his best work. Kawakami Tetsutarō acclaimed parts of 'Cloudy

Autumn' as Nakahara's supreme achievement. The 1967 Kadokawa edition of Nakahara's collected works filled six volumes.

A quintessentially modern poet, Nakahara was also quintessentially Japanese. He possessed an unerring ear for his native language: the literary historian Katō Shūichi has written that 'Probably there is no modern Japanese poet who has better realized the auditory possibilities of the language.' (*A History of Japanese Literature*, Vol. 3, English edition, London, 1983) But he also evoked the abiding genius of the national sensibility, not by harping on the classical literary tradition, nor by any appeal to the geisha-and-cherry-blossom school of atavistic kitsch, but by the very character of his verse. Nakahara's sensitivity to nature and the seasons, reflected in the great number of poem titles that record a time of day or year or particular weather, combined with scenic, undiscursive presentation learned from the Symbolists. This affinity to the concrete moment shaded into an awareness of mood and a devotion to subjective impulses, Keats' 'holiness of the heart's affections', of a kind also regarded as especially Japanese. Perhaps more than any other poet of his time, Nakahara cherished the autonomy of *kokoro*, the heart and its sentiments, and in this he was again at one with the native tradition. His wistfulness, his nostalgia, as well as his sharp urbanity and unintellectualized worldliness, recall much in the nation's literary past. And by this mixture of old with new, revitalizing tradition and maturing novelty, he crafted some of the most sadly beautiful Japanese poems of the century.

A Note on Translation

This book was devised to introduce Nakahara Chūya to English-speaking audiences as a poet; not to act as an adjunct to school or university Japanese courses. Consequently, the main priority in translation has been to produce versions of Nakahara's poems which function as tolerable English verse; generally by concentrating on the progression of imagery and argument at the expense of metrical and sound values. This has done particular violence to the syllabic basis of the verse, generally held to be one of Nakahara's great poetic strengths, but the differences between Japanese and English make this virtually irreproducible in longer poems. Word order has been reproduced where possible, and where it was necessary to switch or invert lines, we attempted to transpose *en bloc*, rather than dicing up the text.

Choice of the poems was dictated chiefly by quality of the originals: hence the selection leans towards the later poems in *Arishi Hi no Uta* at the expense of the earlier works in *Yagi no Uta* and the uncollected poems.

Some of Nakahara's images and metaphors may strike the Western reader as strange. Notes have been provided wherever helpful, but in general this strangeness is not a product of any culture gap, nor of the translation process. It is Nakahara's own.

Goat Songs

山羊の歌

Spring Day's Evening

A zinc roof is eating a rice cracker;[1]
the spring day's evening is mild.
Thrown underarm, ash blanches;
the spring day's evening is calm.

Ah! Is there no scarecrow? – There's none!
Do the horses neigh? – They don't even neigh!
Only, just as moonlight diffuses,
is the spring day's evening docile?

Calm in the field, the temple is crimson;
the wagon wheel   has lost its oil;
when I say something in the historical present,
scorn, scorn   from the skies and mountains.

One rooftile worked loose:
from now on, the spring day's evening,
without a word,   will make its way
into   its own veins.

Moon

This evening the moon, more and more sad,
opens its eyes wide with a foster-father's mistrust.
Time flows, a silver wave in the desert;
an old man's earlobes glow phosphorescent.

Ah, a forgotten canal bank,
left in my heart, a tank's rumbling;
taking a cigarette from a rusty can,
the moon smokes lugubriously.

Around it seven sylphs
are carrying on a heelpoint dance;
to the ignoble moon's heart

they give no solace.
Scattered in the distance, hey, stars, stars!
  – the moon awaits your execution.

Circus

There were several eras;
   there were brown wars.

There were several eras;
   in winter, gales blew.

There were several eras;
   tonight here's a spree,
     tonight here's a spree.

The circus tent's high rafters —
   up there is a swing,
a half-glimpsed swing.

Upside down hands dangling
   under the dirty cotton roof;
yu-an, yu-yon, yu-ya-yu-yon.[1]

The white lamp close by
   exhales cheap ribbon.

The audience are all sardines:
   throats whistle like oyster shells,
yu-an, yu-yon, yu-ya-yu-yon.

      Outside it's pitch black, black on
        black;
      night steadily wears on.
      The fool parachute's nostalgia;
      yu-an, yu-yon, yu-ya-yu-yon.

Spring Night

In a tarnished silver window-frame, peacefully,
   a spray of flowers, peach-coloured flowers.

Fainting from the moonlight,
   the garden earth a beauty spot.[1]

Ah, nothing matters, nothing matters;
   trees, play your parts discreetly.

In this desultory sound,
   no hope...then again, neither repentance.

Only a carpenter who reveres mountains
   can, in a dream, faintly discern a caravan's footsteps.

Inside the window, freshly, dimly,
   sand-coloured silk garments.

The trembling heart's piano sounds;
   no ancestors, parents also vanished.

A buried dog somewhere;
   gushing out in saffron colour,
     spring night!

Morning Song

On the ceiling,   reddish
    light leaked through   the chink in the door,
redolent of   rustic martial music;
    my hands have nothing to turn to.

The small birds' song   is inaudible,
    the sky today   is a pale indigo;
the weary   man's heart
    — no-one   would reproach it.

The morning is vexed   with the odour of resin;
    lost,   the various dreams;
the serried woods   sound in the wind.

A sprawling,   flat sky;
    along the embankment,   melting away...
the beautiful,   various dreams.

The Hour of Death

The autumn sky is a dull grey,
a gleam in the eyes of a black horse;
   the water dries up, the lily wilts,
   ah,   the heart is empty.

Without gods, without guidance,
by the window a woman has passed on;
   the white sky is blind,
   the white wind is cold.

When at the window she washed her hair,
her arm was tender.
   Morning sun pouring down,
   the water dripping.

The streets are loud,
children's voices tangle.
   And so, what will   this soul become?
   Fading away,   will it become sky?

Summer Night in the City

Moon in the sky like a medal,
street-corner buildings like an organ;
debauched men go home singing.
 - Their wing collars are awry -

Their mouths are wide open,
their hearts somehow sad.
Heads turning to dark clods,
just singing - la la - they go.

Business and ancestors,
they hardly forget them;
summer night in the city wearing on -

Deepening to dead gunpowder,
in their eyes the streetlamps blur;
just singing - la la - they go.

One Day in Autumn

On a morning like this, late risers
are drowned in the siren-haunted sea
by the sound of doors banging in the wind and wheels.

The summer night-stalls' chatter and
the architect's conscience are no more.
Everything is ancient history and
the colour of an eye beyond a horizon of granite.

This morning everything is docile under consular flags;
autumn knows nothing but tin and plazas and heaven's
    drumrolls.
Ignoring a mollusc's husky voice,
a purple crouching shadow in the park, an infant puts sand
    in its mouth.

  (A pale blue platform, and
   noisy girls and sneering Yankees;
   Hateful! Hateful!)

Thrusting my hands into my pockets,
walking through the alley, coming out on the wharves,
I meet Today's soul:
I shall pick rags, or some such.

Dusk

On the pond's troubled, murky face,
gathered lotus leaves tremble.
As the lotus leaves are coy,
they hardly make a sound above a whisper.

When they make a sound my heart trembles,
my eyes trace the dim horizon...
the dark, dark mountains merely loom.
– Once lost, things never return.

Nothing could be as sad as this;
the grass roots' smell wafts gently to my nostrils,
the field's earth and stones together looking at me.

– In the end, I'm not willing to plough!
Standing absent-minded in the dusk;
somehow, when Father's image sticks in my mind, I only
   advance a step or two.

Midnight Thought

It's foaming calcium
drying,
sharp – a wilful girl's tearful voice;
the bagshop lady's evening snot.

Forest dusk is
a nebulous mother.
The treetops where insects circle,
a child's dummy's comic dance.

No sign of the hunting dogs with flowing hair,
the stooping hunter turns away.
The meadow close by the wood
    slopes off!

On the black beach Margaret walks up
with her veil blown by the wind.
Her body shall plunge into
a sea that is a solemn god's father!

Above her, on the cliffs,
spirits trace mysterious lines.
Her memory is a sad study's clearout;
soon she must die.

Rainy Winter's Night

Shrouding the wintry black night,
torrential rain was falling.
– Thrown into relief under twilight, the withered rootcrop's
   gloom,[1]
even that was better –
Now, shrouding the black winter's night,
torrential rain is falling.
Even dead virgins' voices cry,
aé ao, aé ao, éo, aéo éo![2]
   Floating in the rain,
vanished some time back, those milk-white bladders...
Now, shrouding the black winter's night,
torrential rain is falling;
my mother's neatly tied sash, too,[3]
washed away in the rainwater, crumpled;
human compassion too
was in the end just the colour of an orange?...

Homecoming

The posts and garden are all dried out;
the weather's fine today.
   Under the floor a spider's web[1]
   is forlornly trembling.

In the mountains even the dead trees breathe;
ah, the weather's fine today.
   The roadside grasses' shadows
   innocently sorrow.

This is my old home;
even a breeze blowing.
   Go on, cry with an open heart,
   a matron's low voice says.

Oh child, what have you done?
– veering, the wind says to me.

Sad Morning

The sound of the rapids rises to the mountains,
the spring light is like stone.
The bamboo pipe's trickle tells a story,
very like a white-haired old woman.

Sung with a mica mouth,
falling backwards, singing;
heart dried up and crumpled,
atop a boulder, balancing.

Unknown flames, going up to the sky!

A rain of echoes, drenching!

...

This way, that way, I clap my hands...

Song of a Summer Day

The blue sky does not move;
there is not a single cloud.
   In the stillness of a summer noon
   the glint of tar, too, becomes pure.

There's something about the summer sky,
something that makes you feel pitiful.
   Scorched brazen-faced sunflowers are
   blooming at the local station.

Like good mothers bringing up children,
the trains' whistles sound
   when running by the mountain.

Running by the mountain,
like mothers, the trains' whistles sound.
In the heat of the summer noon.

Autumn in a Port Town

The sun shines on the stone cliff,
the autumn sky is as beautiful as can be.
In the distance, the port looks
almost as if it has a snail's horns.

In the town, folk are cleaning long pipes.[1]
The rooftiles stretch,
the sky is split.
Officials' holiday – on with the dressing gowns.[2]

'When I am reborn...'
a sailor sings.
'See saw, see saw,'
an old crone sings.

An autumn day in a port town is
a gentle madness.
On that day, in my life,
I lost a chair.[3]

Sigh
(to Kawakami Tetsutarō)[1]

The sigh would go out to the night marsh,
glimmering in the miasma.
That glimmer, malignantly drifting, would: Snap!
The trees would look like the scruff of young scholars'
   necks.

When dawn broke on the horizon, the window would
   open.
The farmer dragging his cart would go towards the town.
Now the sigh would deepen,
like the sound of the cart echoing through the hills.

The foothill pine sticking up in the field would gaze at me,
frank but unsmiling, like an uncle.
It looks as if God is catching fish at the bottom of the
   stratosphere.

When the sky clouded over, locusts' eyes would peer from
   the sandy loam.
In the distance, the town looks like chalk.
Peter the Great's eyes are shining in the clouds.

18

Hangover

Morning, dull light shining,
  and there is wind.
Thousands of cherubs
  playing basketball.

I close my eyes:
  sad drunkenness.
Already the defunct stove
  is whitely rusting.

Morning, dull light shining,
  and there is wind.
Thousands of cherubs
  playing basketball.

Boyhood

The summer sun shone down on blue-black stones,
the garden earth was sleeping in vermilion.

On the horizon, vapour rising
was like omens of the end of the world.

The wheat field where the wind beat roaring
was dim and grey.

Like shadows cast by flying clouds
passing over the field's face, an ancient giant's countenance —

the summer afternoon
when some were napping,
I was running in the fields.

I was champing hope between my teeth;
I despaired, with dazzled eyes...
ah, alive, I was alive!

Little Sister

Night, a beautiful soul crying
  – she is righteous, but –
night, a beautiful soul crying;
  'I don't mind dying now,' it said.

The night wind blowing
over the wet field's black earth, short grass;
'I don't mind dying; I don't mind dying'
the beautiful soul cried.

Night, the sky was high, the wind blowing was tender
  – I could do nothing but pray...

Self-Portrait on a Cold Night

It may not be costly, but
I won't let go of this single rein,
passing through this gloomy region!
Since that intent has clarified
I don't grieve over the winter's night,
only the sorrow of people's frustration.
The humming of women led by longing
I feel as my venial sin,
I let it pierce my skin.

Though I stagger, I keep the peace;
I admonish my indolence
with something of a sense of formality
as I go under the cold winter's moon.

Cheerful, serene, and not selling out,
that's what my soul desired!

Tree Shade

A shrine gate in the light,
elm leaves tremble slightly;
a summer noon's green shade
soothes my remorse.

Dark remorse,   always lingering remorse.
Filled with stupid laughter, my past
soon became tearful darkness,
soon became deep-rooted fatigue.

So now, from morning to night,
I have no life beyond endurance.
Without resentment, as if I had swooned,
my eyes turn skyward.

A shrine gate in the light,
elm leaves tremble slightly;
a summer noon's green shade
soothes my remorse.

Lost Hope

Vanishing into the dark sky,
   my young days' blazing hope.

Like a summer night's star, even now
   visible far off in the sky, even now.

Vanishing into the dark sky,
   my young days' dreams and hope.

Now, here, falling prone
   like a beast, with dark feelings.

Some day those dark feelings
   will clear, and no way of knowing when;

Like drowning in the night's sea,
   seeing the moon in the sky.

The waves are so deep,
   the moon is so pure;

Sad, my young days' blazing hope
   already vanishing into the dark sky.

Image

I

Wind blowing through the pine trees;
the sound of trodden gravel was forlorn.
The warm wind bathed my forehead;
my thoughts were far away, yearning.

When I sat down,
the waves' sound was supernally clear.
There were no stars,
the sky was dark cotton wool.

In a boat I chanced to pass,
a boatman said something to his wife
 — I couldn't catch the words.

The waves' sound was supernally clear.

II

Over every extinguished past,
tears gush out.
The castle wall is dessicated;
the wind blows.

The grass waves;
over the hills, across the fields
no rest;
white angels' countenances do not appear.

Alas I wish to die;
alas I wish to live;
alas I, over every extinguished past,
let tears gush out.
Out of the sky
the wind blows.

Michiko[1]

Your bosom is like the sea,
expansively running inshore.
Faroff sky, blue waves,
even a cool breeze blowing,
sweeping across the pinetops;
the beach whitely stretches away.

And in your eyes that sky's
very end is mirrored.
Waves advancing in line, shore waves,
rapidly moving in.
No time to see, full sail, reefed sail,
charmed by the boat offshore.

And the beauty of that brow
suddenly surprised by the noise of things
awakening from a daytime dream
and, like an ox, naïve,
light and at the same time gentle,
raised, and prostrated.

Childlike, your nape is like a rainbow;
powerless, with arms like a baby's;
strings and voice together, with swift tunes, when you
    dance;
the sea, poignant gold, brims with sunset,
further off the open ocean quietly flourishes;
in the sky, I foresee your demise.

Soiled Sorrow

Soiled sorrow:
today too snow falls on it;
soiled sorrow:
today too wind blows on it.

Soiled sorrow
is like, say, a fox's fur;
soiled sorrow,
covered with snow, curls up.

Soiled sorrow
has no desires or wishes;
soiled sorrow
in its torpor dreams of death.

Soiled sorrow
frightens me piteously;
soiled sorrow
can't be remedied, and the sun sets...

Miscreant's Song
(to Abe Rokurō)[1]

My life, too soon taken in hand
by clumsy gardeners, is sad![2]
Thanks to that, most of my blood
rises to my head, seething, boiling over.

Uneasy, impatient,
always seeking something in the outside world.
Such behaviour is foolish,
such thoughts are hard to understand.

Thus, this pitiful tree,
tough bark, in the sky and wind,
my heart always sinking in mourning thoughts;

my mien is indolent, fitful,
susceptible to others, liable to flatter; thus,
despite myself, I do the stupidest things.

Autumn

1

The field which was burning until yesterday
today stretches away blankly under the cloudy sky.
With each shower the autumn deepens, people say;
late cicadas are already singing everywhere,
in a single tree in the grass.

I smoke a cigarette. The smoke
rises meandering in the stagnant air.
I want to gaze at the horizon and I can't,
for the wraiths of heatwaves keep standing up and sitting
    down
— I end up squatting.

Tinged a dull gold, the sky is overcast — just as usual —
because it's so high, I bow my head.
I am living resigned to fatigue;
the tobacco has three different tastes.
Death already may not be far off...

2

"Well then, goodbye, he said,[1]
unusually full of smiles, with something of a brassy glitter,
and then out he went by that door.
That smile somehow wasn't the smile of a living person,
    you see.

That man's eyes had a colour something like bog water
    when it clears.
When he was speaking, he looked like he was thinking of
    something else.

Cut short his sentences habitually.
And he remembered trivial things down to the last detail."

"Oh, that's right — He knew he was going to die?
When he look at the stars, he said laughing that the stars
    would become me, only recently
...
Only recently, he said of his shoes, 'these certainly aren't
    mine.'"

3

The grass was not trembling at all;
above it butterflies were flying.
Wearing a nightgown, he was standing on the verandah
    watching them.
From here I was watching his actions.
He gazed hard at the yellow butterflies.
You could hear *tōfu* vendors' horns everywhere;[1]
that telegraph pole stood out against the evening sky.
    — Me, he said, turning towards me,
yesterday I lifted a rock weighing nearly fifteen stone.[2]

    — My...why, where? I asked him.
Just then, he gazed deep into my eyes,
like he was angry; my, I was so scared.

People are strange just before they die, aren't they...

Shambolic Town Elegy
(to Sekiguchi Takakatsu)[1]

Preface

Abominable memories,
away! And the old
pitiful feelings and
open heart,
come back!

    Today is Sunday;
    the sun shines on the verandah.
    − Once more taken by Mother
    on the day of the festival, I want her to buy me a balloon;
    the sky was blue, everything was sparkling and
        glittering...

    Abominable memories,
    away!
      Away!

II   *Drunken Life*

My green youth too passed away,
− this cold dawn's cockcrow!
My green youth too passed away.

Surely I have been living without regard for the
    consequences...
Was I too carefree?
− a simple soldier, my heart!

Nevertheless, I detest
people who live only for externals.
Paradoxical human life.

Now, here, laid low by wounds,
 – this cold dawn's cockcrow!
Ah, in the frost this continual cockcrow . . .

III   *Soliloquy*

It's important to carry the vessel
without disturbing the water in the vessel,
While doing so,
the motion should be great.

However, to do so
when there is no chance to find a way,
the heart
must humbly wait on God's benison.

IV

A really pale day today,
rain falling sorrowfully, heavily;
through the air paler than water
the wood releases a sweet aroma.

Deeply autumnal, today
is like stony echoes.
I don't even have memories:
so much less should there be dreams.

Truly, I have lived like stone,
like shadow...
When I try to call, no words;
like the sky, no end.

So sad, my heart;
with nothing to say, I make a fist;
should I blame someone?
This is the worst distress.

Snowy Dusk

The snow falling on my blue felt hat
is bygone hands, or whispering
                              (Hakushū)[1]

The snow falling on the hotel roof
is bygone hands, or whispering;

   The chimney belches smoke,
   and red sparks leap up.

This evening the sky is so dark;
from the dark sky, falling snow...

   Gone at last, that woman,
   I wonder what she's doing now.

Gone at last, that woman,
I wonder if she'll come back soon.

   I'm quietly drinking;
   remorse on remorse, and I feel unsettled.

Quietly, quietly drinking;
regrets stirred up...

   The snow falling on the hotel roof
   is bygone hands, or whispering;

The chimney belches smoke,
and red sparks leap up.

A Song of Childhood

I

Infancy

Above me the falling snow
was like cotton floss.

Boyhood

Above me the falling snow
was like sleet.

17-19

Above me the falling snow
scattered like hail.

20-22

Above me the falling snow
seemed like hailstones.

23

Above me the falling snow
looked like a heavy snowstorm.

24

Above me the falling snow
became very quiet...

II

Above me the falling snow
falls like petals;
there is the crackle of burning wood
when the frozen sky grows dark.

Above me the falling snow,
most tender beloved,
hands outstretched, was falling.

Above me the falling snow,
dropping on a hot forehead,
was like tears.

To the snow above me, falling,
I expressed deep, sincere gratitude; to God
I prayed for long life.

Above me the falling snow
was deeply chaste.

Now is the Time

Voici venir les temps où vibrant sur sa tige
Chaque fleur s'évapore ainsi qu'un encensoir.
                    (Baudelaire, *Harmonie du Soir*)

Now is the time when each flower exhales like a censer;
the air is vague:
dripping flowers and water's sound
and people hurrying home.

Well, Yasuko, now is the time,
quietly together, shall we go down?
In the faraway sky, even the flying birds
are filled with a childlike compassion.

Well, Yasuko, now is the time,
when the sun sets behind the fence and the ultramarine
sky peacefully flows.

Well, Yasuko, now is the time,
your hair ripples in pliant waves.
Each flower exhales like a censer.

Song of the Sheep
(to Yasuhara Yoshihiro)[1]

I *Prayer*

At the hour of death, I will go!
This small chin will grow even smaller!
Because I sense that, for what I did not feel,
I will be punished, and death will draw near.
Ah, at that time, I will go!
At least at that time, I too will be one who feels
  everything!

II

Intention, thou art old dark vapour;
begone from my heart!
I now hope for nothing more than simplicity and peaceful
  murmurs
and, at any rate, neatness.

Society, thou art indulgence of gloomy filth;
do not wake me up again!
I now will try to endure solitude,
my arms already seem like useless things.

Thou, eyes opening wide in suspicion,
eyes not moving for a while as they open.
Ah, heart that believes too much in what is outside itself.

Intention, thou art old dark vapour;
begone from my heart! Begone!
Apart from my poor dreams, nothing interests me.

III

Ma jeunesse ne fut qu'un ténébreux orage,
traversé çà et là par de brillants soleils
(Baudelaire, *L'Ennemi*)

There was a nine-year-old child;
she was a girl-child.
It was as if all the air in the world was hers
and as if that air was something you could lean on.
And on it she leaned her head
when she was talking to me.

I was sitting at the table,[1]
she was sitting on the floor.
The winter morning was unusually mild.
There was lots of sunshine in my room;
and when she leaned her head
the sunlight shone through her earlobes.

She trusted me completely, confided in me completely,
her heart was the colour of an orange;
that tenderness did not overflow,
nor did it cringe away, like a deer.
I forgot everything I was doing;
that time was the only time I savoured.

IV

For all that, my truly desolate heart,
night after night, alone in a rented room,
thinking thoughtless thoughts, monotonous,
my humble heart's duet...

When I hear the train's whistle,
I think of travel, and I think of childhood days;
no, no, I think neither of childhood nor of travel,
only of something *like* travel or childhood...

39

My heart thinks thoughtless thoughts,
shut up, like a box gathering must;
whitened lips, dry cheeks
in this cold-hearted dead silence become sodden...

Because I am used to this, I can endure;
since this loneliness is distressing, without
knowing, in a way accidentally,
come flowing tears, not the tears of love...

The Voice of Life

I am already fed up with Bach and Mozart,
and completely fed up with that happy, easy-going jazz.
I am living like an iron bridge under a cloudy sky after rain.
I am pressed by things forever desolate.

I am not completely quiet in the midst of that desolation.
I am seeking something, always seeking something
in the midst of this terrible immobility, but also terribly
    impatient.
For the sake of this, my appetites and lusts are as nothing.

However, what that thing is, I don't know, I have never
    known;
I don't think there are two, I think there is only one.
However, what that thing is, I don't know, I have never
    known.
Even one way or another to get there, I don't know at all.

Like when I tease myself, I ask myself sometimes:
Is it a woman? Is it a sweet? Is it glory?
Then my heart screams: That's not it; This isn't it; That's
    not it; This isn't it!
Then is it the sky's song, morning, high in the sky, the
    echoing sky's song?

II

No matter what, it is indescribable!
Sometimes I want to explain it briefly, but
since it's inexplicable, indescribable, I believe my life is
    worth living.
That's reality! Unsullied happiness! Anything anyhow is
    good!

Everyone, no matter if they know it or not, aspires after
    this,
even though it is not as plain as victory and defeat;
it's like a pleasant absent feeling known by all, desired by
    all;
everyone as long as they live in this world cannot desire it
    wholly!

If happiness is like this, like the limit of unselfishness,
if it is a thing these cunning merchants call 'Fool',
if so, this world in which one cannot live without eating,
I must say, is unfair.

But all the same, that's the world;
here we live, it's not arbitrary injustice;
since that is the principle on which we are constituted,
since it is so, then thinking there is no such extreme in the
    world, it's better for the moment to have peace of mind.

III

Then, in short, it's a question of passion.
Thou, if thou art angry from the bottom of thy heart,
    be angry!

Then thy anger,
even before thy ultimate aim,
never, never neglect it!

That is, your passion will run for a time, then stop, but
the public effect will persist
and obstruct the reform of your future conduct.

IV

Evening, under the sky; if you feel your body one speck,
    you will not mind about anything.

42

Songs of Past Days

在りし日の歌

Shame
– A Song of Past Days –

Why is it I feel this shame;
autumn is a mountain's shadow on a day of white wind.
In the pasania's leaf litter,
unnaturally mature trunks burst forth;

branches, intertwined, seem sad;
the sky is filled with dead children's spirits, twinkling;
just then over yonder above the fields
astrakhan interwoven became a dream of ancient
    mammoths.

In the pasania's leaf litter,
unnaturally mature trunks burst forth;
that day, between those trunks, intimate eyes,
sisterly colour, you were there.

That day, between those trunks, intimate eyes,
sisterly colour, you were there.
Ah! Past days' low flames flare up from time to time;
my heart, why, oh why, this shame.

Late Evening Rain
– Image after Verlaine –

The rain, this evening, like long ago;
    singing a song still like long ago.
Maundering, maundering, terribly stubborn;
    then I see Monsieur Ver, that hulk,
going down the alleys between the warehouses.

Between the warehouses his slicker gleams.
    And then the peat's miserable comedy.
Well, if only I go through this alley,
    if only I go through, there is a faint hope...
Oh! This is really hope?

I will have nothing to do with cars,
    I will have even less to do with streetlamps.
The bar lantern's rotting eyeball:
    far off its chemistry sounds.

Early Spring Wind

Today all day, again golden wind,
  in the big wind, silver bells;
today all day, again golden wind,

  Like a queen's crown.
  I sit down at my desk,
facing the open window.

  The wind blowing outside is a golden wind;
  in the big wind, silver bells;
today all day, again golden wind.

  The dry grass's sound is sad;
  smoke dissipates in the sky;
the shade gaily flirts.

  The deep brown earth smells sweet;
  the washing poles go up to the sky;
the rising slope eases, but

  like a green woman's chin
  the hill's treetops bristle;
today all day, again golden wind.

Blue Eyes

1 *Summer Morning*

In my sad heart the day breaks,
   in my glad heart the day breaks.
No! What's going on?
   Indeed the sad day breaks.

The blue eyes didn't move,
   the whole world was still sleeping;
then "that time" was about to pass.
   Ah, a remote, remote story.

The blue eyes didn't move:
   – now maybe they're moving...
The blue eyes didn't move,
   pitiful and beautiful!

Here I am now, in the yellow light.
   After that I don't know what happened...
Ah, so "the time" was about to pass,
   like blue vapour gushing out.

2 *Winter Morning*

After that what became of it...
that I didn't know;
anyway, in the morning, from the misty airport
the airplanes had vanished for good.
Left behind, only cruel gravel and weeds
and cheek-piercing cold remained.
– Even on this kind of cruel vast morning,
one must meet others wearing a smile,
which I thought was a truly pitiable thing;
however, there still
were those who were so full of smiles,
feeling superior.
The sun shone in the mist, the frost on the grassblades
 thawed,
from faroff houses cocks crowed;
the mist and the light and the frost and the cocks
touched no-one's heart.
Everyone had gone home, seated at table.
 (What was left in the airport was me,
 trying to kick an empty cigarette packet.)[1]

A Three-Year-Old's Memory

On the verandah, the sun is shining
while the resin sleeps in five colours;
a garden with one persimmon tree;
loquat-coloured earth; the flies whine.

On the toilet, I was being held:
then, from my arse, an insect dropped down;
because that insect was wriggling in the toilet's shallows,
because it was wriggling, I was amazed.

Ah, I was so scared,
somehow unbelievably scared.
Then, for some time, I
made myself cry and cry.

Ah, I was scared, scared
– inside the house there was silence.
Next Door had flown up and away!
Next Door had flown up and away!

June Rain

Again for some time,   morning rain;
iris-coloured,   green;
eyes moist,   a long-faced woman
appears   and vanishes.

As she appears   and vanishes,
sunk in sorrow,   drizzling and
falling in   the field,
falling   without end.

Beat the drum,   blow the pipe,
innocent child,   Sunday,
playing on   the mat.

Beat the drum,   blow the pipe,
as he plays,   rain falls,
outside the window frame,   rain falls.

Rainy Day

In the street the rain is pouring down;
the houses' baseboards are old.
All kinds of mocking eyes are growing gentle;
I wake in the middle of a dream of petals.

*

A brown sword's sheath,
a tongue-tied friend,
your forehead was square.
I remember you.

*

The rasp of a file, hoarse-voiced;
a tired, aging stomach;
in the rain, listen: far off,
tender, tender lips.

*

Brick-coloured frustrations
glimpsed intermittently in the rainy sky.
A bright girl's black hair, and
a doting father's head, and a beloved...

Spring

Spring makes the earth and the grass sweat afresh.
To dry the sweat, the lark mounts to the sky.
This morning the tiled roof has no complaints.
From the long schoolhouse the chorus ascends to the sky.

Ah, peaceful, peaceful.
It's come round, this is my spring this year.
The hope which long ago set my heart trembling, today
grown grave and deep blue, out of the sky falls on me.

So I will end up witless, end up stupid.
– Behind the bush, is it a stream, or silver, or ripples?
Behind the bush, is it a stream, or silver, or ripples?

The big cat shakes its head clumsily,
rolling a bell,
trying to roll a bell.

Song of a Spring Day

Flow, fleeting modesty!
Flowing away to the sky's country?
And my heart scattered far and wide.
My Egyptian cigarette's smoke drifts.

Flow, hiding cold cares;
flowing away to the foothills?
Somewhere you can see the unseen
face's mysterious gorge...

In an afternoon nap's opulent dream,
above the field's sky's sky?
Does it howl, howl!

The yellow barn and white storehouse;
over where you can see the waterwheel,
is it flowing, flowing away?

Summer Night

Ah, in my tired heart
a cherry-pink woman   passes by,
a woman passes by.

In the summer night the paddy field's sludge,
resentment has faded away.
 − Will the surrounding mountains' seasons come round?

Barefoot is gentle, the sand is beneath;
open eyes   are left behind;
the hazy night sky   is high and dark.

The hazy night sky is high and dark;
nothing can be done about parental love.
 − In my tired heart,   a petal passes by.

In my tired heart,   a petal passes by;
from time to time a gong grazes the writings.
The mist is lovely, but hot!

Young Beast's Song

Dark night in a field of deep grass;
a beast in a jar,
striking flint, made stars;
mixing winter, the wind moaning.

Then, the beast didn't look at anything
apart from castanets and moonlight,
cuddling the stars that never awoke,
inside the jar, receiving blasphemy.

Memory became a lamp like after rain,
hugging the wind's shoulders, waving.
Ah, a bewitching tale –
and the slave became as beautiful as a queen.

    The young prince's smile like an eggshell and
    the dull-witted child's white blood cells
    in their way made the beast scared.

In the dark night, in the field of deep grass,
a beast's heart was smouldering.
In the dark night, in the field of deep grass –
In antiquity, even soliloquy was beautiful...!

This Infant

When sprites come and go in the sky,[1]
in the field,
livid,
this infant.

When black clouds draw lines in the sky,
this infant,
squeezed-out tears are
silver liquid...

I hope the world will split in two,
and I hope one side will drift away;
then I will sit down on the other side,
the blue sky alone –

Granite boulders,
the seashore sky,
the temple roof and
the edge of the sea...

Winter Day's Remembrance

A child who, in the cold wind, took a sparrow in his hand
    and petted it,
in the night, suddenly died.

Next morning was frosty.
That child's big brother went to send a telegram.

In the night, still Mother cried.
Father went on an ocean voyage.

What became of the sparrow, no-one knew.
The north wind made the street white.

When the well bucket bumped,
Father's answering telegram arrived.

Day after day the frost came down.
Father still could not return from his ocean voyage.

After that, how did Mother do...?
Big brother who sent the telegram was scolded at school
    today.

Autumn Day

Behind a line   of trees   running beside   the riverbed,
autumn is   a beautiful   woman's   eyelid
   looking as if   about to cry,   the sky's   moisture,
long ago,   a horse's   hoofbeats.

Because of   long years'   fatigue,
when I go   along the highway   autumn imbues   my body;
   it's nothing   at all,   just nothing   at all,
even my pattens'   clop   imbues   my body.[1]

Now the sun   illuminates   half   the watercourse,
on the stream   invisible   rafts   pass by;
   though the fields   beyond   repose.

My boon   companion's   foolish   manner
somehow   mingles   with   the air.
Autumn is   concern   with lips   pursed.

Cold Night

In the winter night
my heart is grieving,
grieving without reason...
my heart is rusty, purple.

Behind the solid door,
old days' abstraction.
On the hilltop,
cotton seeds burst open.

Here the firewood smoulders,
the smoke, as if it
knows itself, ascends.

Without being invited,
without wanting to,
my heart smoulders...

Winter Daybreak

The snow lying on the rooftiles is a touch hard,
the dead trees' twigs are sleepy like a deer;
six o'clock on a winter morning,
my head too is sleepy.

The birds pass by singing –
the garden earth is sleepy like a deer.
 – The wood has fled, the farmhouse has fled.
The sky is sad weakness.
  My heart is sad...

By and by a faint light shines,
the blue sky is opening.
In the sky above Above, the god Jupiter's hand-drum
  sounds.
 – The mountains of the four quarters subside.

The farmhouse garden yawns,
the road greets the sky.
  My heart is sad...

Let Old People
– [Void Autumn] Number Twelve[1]

Let old people be at peace,
so that they can repent to the full.

I wish to repent,
to the full, because repentance eases my soul.

Ah, I wish to weep interminably;
forgetting Father, Mother, brothers, friends and complete
   strangers;
like the dawn sky, like the evening wind wafted over hills,
like flying streamers, I will weep.

As if once more parting words' echoes rise to the clouds,
   resounding across the fields,
mingling with the wind over the sea, endlessly passing
   away...

Envoi

Ah, through cowardice, for a long time, a really long time,
we have busied ourselves with vanities, have forgotten to
   cry, really forgotten to cry...

On the Lake

When the moon pops out,
we'll push the boat out.
The waves will come lapping against the side,
and there'll be a little wind.

When we're offshore, it'll be dark;
the water dripping from the oars
will murmur intimately
– when your words break off.

The moon will prick up its ears
and come down a little;
when we kiss,
the moon will be over our heads.

And you'll say more
senseless things and sulky words;
I'll listen without missing a single one
– but without breaking stroke.

When the moon pops out,
we'll push the boat out.
The waves will come lapping against the side,
and there'll be a little wind.

Winter Night

Everybody, tonight is peaceful,
the kettle is boiling;
I care for a woman,
I have no woman.

And so I have no worries;
in fantasies like the indescribably
resilient air,
I picture that woman.

The indescribably resilient,
perfectly clarified night's silence;
hearing the kettle boil,
I am dreaming a woman.

And so, the night advances, the night deepens;
the winter night when only dogs are awake,
shadows and cigarettes and me and dogs,
is an indescribable cocktail.

2

There is nothing better than the air;
and at that there is nothing better than the air indoors on a
    cold night.
There is nothing better than smoke;
there is nothing merrier than smoke.
By and by you will come to know it;
the time will come when you will agree.

There is nothing better than the air.
In the cold night like a bony matron's hand,
like that hand's resilience   soft   and hard,
like hardness   like that hand's resilience,
like smoke   like that woman's passion,
like burning   like vanishing,
there is nothing better than the air   indoors on a cold
    night.

Autumn News

Linen, in the morning, runs after human skin,
sparrows' voices have hardened;
chimney smoke is scattered about in the wind.

It's as if when you dig up volcanic ash there's ice:
at the bottom of the crystal empyrean, the blue sky
sinks cold, deep.

As I sunbathe
on the cathedral's stone steps:
abiding in the sun, flowers, and
beyond, the aimless chorus of insects.

The autumn day warms my body,
my hands and feet are chilled;
and now an ad balloon rises and drifts
in the sky over Shinjuku.[1]

Bone

Look, look, it's my bone!
breaking through the lifelong troubles
of that corrupted flesh,
washed bare by the rain,
sticking out, the bone's tip.

It's not even shiny,
its indifference futile,
absorbing the rain,
blown by the wind,
just reflecting the sky.

In its lifetime
in the restaurant's bustle
where it used to sit
where it used to munch boiled greens[1]
it seemed so funny.

Look, look, it's my bone –
Is it me looking at it? It's funny.
Its soul still lingering
has come back to the bone,
for a look perhaps?

On the old home stream's bank,
standing in half-withered grass
is it...me looking?
High as a signboard,
the bone, bare, sticks out.

Autumn Day's Frenzy

I no longer have anything;
I have nothing at all in my hands;
moreover, I don't even regret it;
more than ever, I have nothing to call my own.

All the same, the weather's fine today;
for some time, many planes have been flying past
— Will Europe start a war or not?
Who knows such things anyway?

The weather's really fine today,
the sky's azure is dim with tears;
the poplars are fluttering, fluttering;
a short while ago the children went to Heaven;

No longer anyone apart from sunbathing
salarymen's wives and travelling cobblers.
The sound of the cobblers' rolling drums
alone glorifies the bright ruins.

Ah, someone please come and help me;
in Diogenes' time at least a little bird must have sung,
but today not even the sparrows are cheeping;
even the shadows cast on the ground are already too faint.

— By the way, where has the country girl gone?
Is that purple dried flower no longer smudged?
Isn't the sun shining on the grass?
Is there no longer even an illusion of Ascension?

What am I saying?
What kind of derangement has touched me?
Where have the butterflies flown to?
Was today not spring, but autumn?

Ah, then I shall drink thick syrup:
make it cool, with a thick straw;
sipping, sipping it without looking round,
desiring nothing, nothing at all...!

Korean Woman

The cords of the Korean woman's clothes
tangle in the autumn wind.
Walking on the highway, every once in a while
she yanks her child's hand:
your face with knitted brows,
your skin tanned like dried fish,
what is that face thinking
– truly I have grown down-at-heel;
perhaps I looked befuddled:
she gazed at me suspiciously,
she hurried the child away...
a little dust was rising,
what should I think;
a little dust was rising,
what should I think...

Spring and the Baby

In the rape field, what sleeps is...
In the rape field, what is windblown is...
Isn't it a baby?

No, what's making a noise is electric wires,
all day buzzing in the sky, electric wires.
What sleeps in the rape field is a baby, though.

What runs by is a bicycle, a bicycle;
the road over there, what runs by
clipping the pale peach-coloured wind...

clipping the pale peach-coloured wind...
what runs by is the rape field and the sky's white clouds
— leaving the baby in the field.

Skylark

All day buzzing in the sky,
ah, electric wires, electric wires!
All day singing in the sky,
ah, clouds' child, skylark!

In the blue, blue sky,
round and round, winkling in,
singing *pii-chikuchiku*,
ah, clouds' child, skylark!

What walks by is the rape field,
towards the horizon, towards the horizon;
What walks by is that mountain, this mountain,
under the blue, blue sky.

What sleeps in the rape field,
in the rape field, what sleeps,
in the rape field blown by the wind,
what sleeps is a baby?

Early Summer Night

The summer has come again this year.
In the night, polar bears made from steam
advance across the marsh.
– There are all kinds of things going on.
I have done all kinds of things,
some of them were happy things, but
looking back, all of them are sad;
like the grating of iron;
everything, having a sense of approaching evening,
childhood, old age, youth, maturity,
together, raising such a poignant yell
under circling moths in the dusk,
has an impermanent poignant chin.
And yet though tonight is a fine June night;
though faroff sounds waft delectably on the wind,
I feel somehow sad;
the just-faded ringing of the iron bridge,
over the great river, over the iron bridge, the sky is a dim
    slaty grey.

North Sea

What lives in the sea
is not mermaids;
what lives in the sea
is only waves.

Under the north sea's cloudy sky,
waves here and there bare their teeth,
cursing the sky.
No-one knows when the curse will expire.

What lives in the sea
is not mermaids;
what lives in the sea
is only waves.

Innocent Song

Thinking about it, I have come far.
That winter evening when I was twelve.
The steam whistle that echoed
in the sky above the port, where is it now?

The moon was between the clouds;
I heard the whistle and,
terrified, shrank back;
then, the moon was in the sky.

Since, how many years have gone by?
Following the whistle's vapour absently
with my eyes, I grew sad.
Where is the person I was then?

Now I have a wife and child;
thinking about it, I have come far.
But hereafter for how long
will I go on living.

I will go on living.
The long days and nights that have passed,
since I long for them so much like this,
somehow I have no self-assurance.

Yet as long as I go on living,
since after all to persevere is my nature,
so it is I feel myself
to be a pitiable thing.

When I think about it,
since after all I will persevere,
sometimes I long for the old days, then
somehow I will get along.

When I consider, it's easy.
In the end it's a question of will.
I must muddle through.
As long as I do that, it's all right,

I think, but nonetheless,
that winter evening when I was twelve.
The steam whistle that echoed
in the sky above the port, where is it now?

Quietude

Nothing visits me;
my heart is quiet.

It was Sunday's roofed school paths,
– everyone gone to the meadow.

The floorboards have a cold shine,
small birds are singing in the garden.

The half-shut tap's
droplet blinks!

The earth is rose-coloured, larks in the sky;
the sky is a beautiful April.

Nothing visits me;
my heart is quiet.

Memories

On a fine day, the open sea,
how beautiful it is!
On a fine day, the open sea
is like gold or silver, isn't it?

By the gold or silver open-sea waves
charmed, charmed, to the end of the cape
I came, but the gold and silver
withdrew further off, shining on the deep.

At the end of the cape was a brickworks,
in the works garden the bricks were being dried;
the drying bricks were red;
and the works didn't let out a sound.

By the brickworks I sat down;
for a while I smoked cigarettes.
Smoking, I whiled away the time
and out at sea the waves were roaring.

Out at sea, the waves were roaring;
I didn't care, whiling away the time.
Whiling away the time, head and body
snugly warmed.

It was snugly warm,
the works on the cape was catching the sun;
the brickworks didn't make a sound,
in the grove beyond birds were singing.

The birds were singing, and the brickworks,
without flinching, rested motionless.
The birds were singing, and the brickworks'
window glass was catching the sun.

Even though the window glass caught the sun,
it didn't look warm at all.
The fine early spring day's
brickworks at the end of the cape!

*

Soon after that the brickworks closed down;
the brickworks has died,
and the brickworks' window glass
must all have been broken.

The brickworks shut and withered;
by the grove, still loitering,
by the grove, still birds singing, but
the brickworks just crumbles.

Out at sea the waves still roar, and
the sun shines on the garden earth, but
no workers come to the brickworks,
I too do not go to the brickworks.

The chimneys that once belched smoke
are now just standing eerily:
especially eerie on rainy days,
somewhat eerie on clear days.

Even the somewhat eerie chimneys that belched
now in any case can't do a thing.
These enormous old soldiers
from time to time feel bitter; their eyes are frightful.

Their eyes are frightful; today too, I
have gone out to the beach, sitting on the stone,
eyes vaguely downcast, pondering.
My heart too ebbs and flows.

The New Year's Bell[1]

The new year's bell rings in the dark, far sky.
For millions of years, shaking the ageold nights'
    air,
the new year's bell rings in the dark, far sky.

The foggy sky over the temple grove...
ringing somewhere there, then comes echoing.
The foggy sky over the temple grove...

At that time, children munch *soba* at their
    parents' knee;[2]
at that time, there are crowds in Ginza, crowds in
    Asakusa.[3]
At that time, children munch *soba* at their
    parents' knee.

At that time, there are crowds in Ginza, crowds in
    Asakusa.
At that time, how do prisoners feel, how do they
    feel?
At that time, there are crowds in Ginza, crowds in
    Asakusa.

The new year's bell rings in the dark, far sky.
For millions of years, shaking the ageold nights'
    air,
the new year's bell rings in the dark, far sky.

Half My Life

I have suffered a great deal.
What kind of suffering it was
I never thought I would tell.
And whether that suffering was worth
something or nothing.
I never even think about such things.

Anyhow, I have suffered.
I have really suffered!
And here, now, before my desk,
I find only myself.
Gazing fixedly at my extended hands
is all I can do.

    Outside, this evening, leaves rustle;
    the faroff feeling of a spring evening.
    So I will die peacefully;
    as I sit, I'm going to die.

Spring Evening's Reflections

The rain stops, the wind blows.
  The clouds flow, hide the moon.
Everyone, tonight's a spring evening.
  The tepid wind blows.

Somehow, a deep sigh,
  somehow, far away, a phantasm
gushes out, but I can't grasp it.
  No-one can tell of it.

No-one can tell of it.
  It is so, but that indeed
is life itself, isn't it?
  though it cannot be revealed...

So human beings, each and every one,
  feeling so in their hearts, when they meet each other
smile sweetly, and such a thing
  is life, which will pass away, won't it?

The rain stops, the wind blows.
  The clouds flow, hide the moon.
Everyone, tonight's a spring evening.
  The tepid wind blows.

Cloudy Sky

One morning   I saw   in   the sky
a black   flag   fluttering
   Fluttering   it was   fluttering   but
I heard   no sound   because of   the height

   I tried   to haul   down   the flag
There was   no rope   so I   couldn't
   the flag   just fluttered   and fluttered
as if   it would go   deeper into   the sky

   Mornings   like this   in my childhood   days
Sometimes   I think   I have   seen them
   Then   it was   over   the fields
and now   over   the city   roofs

   Then   and now   though time   has gone by
here   there   though the place   has changed
   fluttering   fluttering   alone   in the sky
even now   unchanged   this   black flag

Feeling for a Dragonfly

A fine   autumn sky
a red dragonfly   is flying
bathed in faint   evening sun.
I am standing   in the field

far off   factory chimneys
are blurred   in the evening sun.
I let out   a deep sigh, and
hunkering down   pick up a stone.

That stone's   coolness
at last   warms in my palm.
I throw it aside   then pull up grass
the grass bathed   in evening sun.

The pulled-up grass   on the earth
just, just   withering;
far off factory   chimneys
are blurred   in the evening sun.

Gone Never to Return
– Kyoto –[1]

I was at the edge of this world. The sun poured down gently, the wind was shaking the flowers.

On the wood bridge, the dust all day in silence; the posts all day crimson and the pram with the pinwheel were always standing in the street.

I couldn't see any residents or children in the street, I didn't have a single relative; my task was to look from time to time at the sky's colour over the weathercock.

Yet I wasn't bored, there was honey in the air; that honey wasn't a substance, it was always fit to eat.

I had tried smoking, but I only enjoyed the smell. Besides, unusually for me, I only smoked outside.

Well, my personal belongings were one towel. Although I had a pillow, there was no sign of the quilt; I also had a toothbrush, but the only book I had, had nothing written in it; from time to time I took it in my hand, and just enjoyed the weight.

The women were yearning, but I never thought to go and see them even once. It was enough to dream of them.

An indescribable something was always driving me on; while I didn't even have an aim, hope was beating in my heart.

*

In the wood, there was the world's most mysterious park; almost uncannily cheerful men, women and children were strolling around; they spoke a language I didn't understand, they expressed feelings I didn't understand.

Well, in that sky, silver cobwebs were sparkling.

A Fairy Tale

One autumn night, far far away,
there were only pebbles of a dry riverbed
on which the sun – rippling,
rippling – was shining.

"Sun", but like silica or something, it seemed,
extremely hard powder, it seemed:
which was why – rippling –
a faint sound arose.

All at once, on the pebbles, a butterfly landed:
pale, yet distinct,
its shadow was cast.

Soon that butterfly vanished; then, unawares,
where till now nothing flowed in the riverbed, water
– rippling, rippling – was flowing...

Phantasm

In my head, since when I'm not sure,
an unhappy pierrot was living;
he dressed in a silk gauze costume
and bathed in the moonlight.

Sometimes he, with effeminate hands,
gestured repeatedly, but
I never understood his meaning, and
I only made him sad.

As he gestured, he moved his mouth, but
it was like watching an old shadow play —
there was no sound at all, and
what he said I didn't understand.

White on him the moonlight glowed;
in the strange bright mist,
his dim figure was slowly moving;
only his eyes all along looked gentle.

Song Without Words

It's in a faraway place, but
here I must wait.
Here the air is thin and blue,
softly pale like a leek root.

I must never hurry,
I must wait here long enough;
I musn't gaze distantly like a girl;
certainly, I should wait here.

Nonetheless, it loomed far off in the evening sun,
thick and thin as a whistle's sound;
but I mustn't dash off that way;
certainly, I must wait here.

If I do that, sometime my burden will ease;
certainly, I will be able to get there for sure,
though it was like chimney smoke
far, far away, forever trailing in the glowing sky.

Beach on a Moonlit Night

On a moonlit night, a button
was left on the strand line.

I picked it up: that it might be useful
hardly occured to me.
Somehow I couldn't bear to throw it away;
I tucked it into my sleeve.[1]

On a moonlit night, a button
was dropped on the strand line.

I picked it up: that it might be useful
hardly occured to me.
   I couldn't throw it at the moon;
   I couldn't throw it at the waves.
I tucked it into my sleeve.

On a moonlit night, the button I picked up
shook me to the fingerends, shook me to the heart.

On a moonlit night, the button I picked up:
how could I throw it away?

Spring Will Come Again[1]

Spring will come again, people say.
Yet I am heartsick.
Nothing will happen when spring comes;
that child will not come again.

I remember May this year:
I bundled you off to the zoo.
When I showed you the elephant, you went: 'Meow';
and when I showed you the birds, again you went: 'Meow'.

The deer I showed you last of all,
its antlers must have impressed you a lot:
you stared at it without saying a thing.

At that time you really were
in the light of this world,
standing and staring at it...

Moonlight

(Part I)

The moon was shining
the moon was shining

    In the garden corner hedge
    hides a dead child.

The moon was shining
the moon was shining

    Look, Tircis and Aminte[1]
    have come out on the lawn.

They've brought a guitar, but
they've just cast it aside.

    The moon was shining
    the moon was shining

Moonlight

(Part II)

Oh, Tircis and Aminte
come out to play in the garden.

Tonight's a real spring eve
and there's a lukewarm haze.

Lit up by the moon
on the garden bench,

the guitar beside them, but
it seems they won't play at all.

Beyond the lawn is a forest,
thick and black.

Oh, Tircis and Aminte;
while they whisper,

in the forest a dead child
crouches like a firefly.

The Village Clock

The big village clock
was working day and night.

The clockface's paint
had already lost its shine.

When I drew near,
there were lots of tiny cracks.

And even the evening sun shining on it
had a mellow hue.

Before it struck the hour,
it wheezed.

Whether it was the face or the clockwork making the noise,
neither I nor anyone else knew.

Chōmon Gorge, Winter[1]

In Chōmon Gorge, the water was flowing.
It was a cold, cold day.

I was at a restaurant,
pouring myself *sake*.

Apart from me,
there were no other guests.

The water, as though a thing with a soul,
was flowing and flowing.

By and by, like an orange, the setting sun
spilled over railings.

Ah! – there was such a time;
it was a cold, cold day.

Midday
Scene: The Marunouchi Building[1]

Ah, the twelve o'clock siren; there's the siren, siren;
streaming, streaming out they come, out they come!
Salarymen's lunchhour, idly, idly swinging their arms;
one after another, out they come, out they come.
The huge building's dark, tiny tiny entrance.
The open sky is hazy, hazy; a little dust rising.
Looking up with strange eyes, or looking down...
only a cherry blossom, cherry blossom.
Ah, the twelve o'clock siren; there's the siren, siren;
streaming, streaming out they come, out they come!
The huge building's dark, tiny tiny entrance.
The siren, blown in the sky, resounds, resounds, and fades
  away.

Spring Day's Caprice

1

When someone you love dies,
you've got to kill yourself.

When someone you love dies,
other than that, there's nothing else to do.

But nonetheless, if your sins are deep
and if you go on living

you should have a sense of service
you should have a sense of service.

Because someone you love has died
certainly has died

because there's no way now
for that one's sake, for that one's sake,

you must have a sense of service
you must have a sense of service.

2

Once you have a sense of service, though
now you can do nothing special,

then, more than ever, you peruse books carefully,
then, more than ever, you are civil to people.

You walk at the correct tempo,
you weave your straw hat piously;

as if you're almost a toy soldier,
as if every day is Sunday.

Strolling in the shrine's patch of sun,
if you chance on an acquaintance, you smile at him;

you make friends with the sweet peddler,
you scatter peanuts for the pigeons;

when you are dazzled, you move into the shade,
you consider the earth and the plants.

The moss is truly cool;
indescribable, this beautiful day.

Worshippers walking in a stream,
and I'm not angry with anything.

(Truly, human life, a momentary dream,
is beautiful as a rubber balloon.)

mounting to the sky, shining, vanishing –
Hi, how are you today?

Long time no see; how are things these days?
Shall we have tea somewhere round here?

We're cheered, but once in the teashop
there's not much to talk about;

gloomily smoking cigarettes,
indescribable resignation –

Outside it's really bustling!
So see you soon, regards to your wife.

When you go abroad, please drop us a line.
You'd better not drink too much.

Coaches passing, trains passing;
truly human life is like a bride.

Dazzling, beautiful, even as she lowers her eyes;
once you've made her speak, will you be let down?

even so, she'll warm your heart;
truly human life is like a bride.

100

3

Well, everyone,
don't be too happy and don't be too sad;
shall we shake hands at the correct tempo?

After all, what's lacking in us,
we understand, is sincerity.

Well then, everyone, well, all together,
shall we shake hands at the correct tempo?

Frogs' Voices

The sky covers the earth:
then here and there on the earth are ponds.
In those ponds tonight frogs are croaking...
– So, what are they croaking?

Are their voices falling from the sky
and disappearing into the sky?

The sky covers the earth,
then the frogs' voices carry across the water's surface.

Well, though this area is too damp;
even these posts we find too dry
for our tired hearts.

Our heads are heavy, our necks stiff.
Well, even so, when the night comes the frogs croak,
their voices carry across the water's surface and reach the
  dark clouds.

Uncollected Poems

未刊詩篇

Self-Portrait on a Cold Night[1]

2

Oh Lover, stop that sad song;
since your soul is fretful,
you sing such a song.
What's more, you're wilfully
singing to our closest friends.

Ah, you shouldn't do that!
Don't catch the sadness as it falls;
feeling easy imaginary rapture is happiness, and
running around looking for shops that sell yourself;
what a sad sadness that is...

3

God, have pity on me please!

Since I am frail,
whenever I come across sadness I cannot support myself,
    and
I exchange my life for words.
Without being either too stiff or
too slovenly,
I've got into a state where it seems I've no way to support
    myself.

God, have pity on me please!
These my frail bones, fill them with a warm tremelo please.
Ah God, before anything else, I can be myself,
so please give me sunlight and work!

Fig Leaves

The fig leaves are thick and dark in the evening sky,
blown by the wind,
through the spaces, sky appears;
like a beautiful, gap-toothed
old woman, the tree has a fine carriage,
standing still in the evening sky.

– And I am disheartened;
my past's confused
piled-up memories,
no way to disentangle them, irritated;
some day, to the tangibility of my head's burdens
I will entrust my body, I will entrust my heart.

Not saying anything
this evening, nape bared to the wind,
looking up at the waving, thick, dark
fig tree's crown.
I try as hard as I can to love
something I don't know.

Cicadas

The cicadas are singing, the cicadas are singing;
other than cicadas singing, there's nothing!
I am dozing, dozing.
...And there is wind...
the sky shows through the pinewoods;
I am dozing, dozing.

"No, that's not it, that's not it," he says.
"That's wrong," I say.
"No, no," he says.
"That's wrong," I say;
then I wake up and, yes, he was someone who died long
    ago...
And then the grave where he rests forever, or some such,
    rises before my eyes...

It is a certain district in the west, called Dry Riverbed:[1]
apart from rainy days, there is no water;
close to the river with its myths
there is a small graveyard in the sandy earth under the
    bushes
 – there too the cicadas must be singing;
flickering, the evening sun shines...

The cicadas are singing, the cicadas are singing;
other than cicadas singing, there's nothing!
My indolence? Am I indolent?
I don't think anything about me!
The cicadas are singing, the cicadas are singing;
other than cicadas singing, there's nothing!

Morning

Bright morning,
purple shadows of things,
cold morning air,
ash-grey shingles,
azure sky,
wind!

Something I can't remember...
a thing dear to my heart,
either down below or far above,
now whistling, a lost whistle;
that whistle whistles sharply,
sharply!

Wind!
Azure sky,
ash-grey shingles,
cold morning air,
bright morning,
purple shadows of things...

Cloudy Autumn

1

One day you will look at me, laughing
because my face is too pale,
blown by the November wind, like fig leaves or something,
like an abandoned dog.

Truly that's how it seems to be:
I may be more wretched than a dog, perhaps;
I myself occasionally thought that way,
I myself might have sorrowed.

In spite of all that you will again remember,
in the time when I am not, on the day when I am no longer
    on this earth,
that man, that time, at that point on that road,
pale-faced, like fig leaves, blown by the wind — it was a
    cold afternoon —

disconsolate, abandoned like a dog.

2

The cat was mewing, when everyone had fallen asleep,
in the nearby lot, in the darkness,
really close, serene and fine-voiced;
serene and fine-voiced, mewing in the dark.

If tonight it so serenely
mews the whole night through,
the cat will surely be living
with a close heart...

So sad and full of yearning,
if this evening it is mewing that way,
somehow my existence too
doesn't seem altogether meaningless...

The cat behind the weeds in the lot,
feeling acutely the pebbles underfoot,
feeling that chill in its feet,
was mewing in the foggy night —

3

Your pipe's
filthiness, its char,
I know too well, yet,
almost uncannily clearly I know, yet...

This evening the lamp smoulders gently;
your and my shadows dimly falling
on the floor or on the walls;
there is the sound of a faroff train.

Your pipe's
filthiness, its char,
I honestly know very well, yet
in the span of eternity, I wonder what will
become of that...

110

This evening my life is smouldering,
your and my lives are smouldering;
I can only think our lives, like tobacco,
are burning swiftly away.

Truly impressions' clarity,
our memories, so to speak our lives' footprints,
are too clear;
what on earth do they mean?

This evening the lamp smoulders gently;
your and my shadows dimly falling
on the floor or on the walls;
there is the sound of a faroff train.

In any case, when aims are uncertain,
resignation becomes courage;
by the way, that aims are absolutely uncertain
is surely impossible.

There my life smoulders gently,
your and my lives are smouldering;
I can only think our lives, like tobacco,
are burning swiftly away.

*

The crickets are singing
the bugle is sounding the last post
trains are still running
it's the witching hour
no, it's not that late yet

that's two hours from now
then, the boy, can he stay awake?
No, the boy should go to bed early
Once he's gone to bed, can he get up later?
In the morning, he can get up
How do you make the morning come?
The morning will come by itself
How and where will it come?
It will wash its face, then come out
Is that tomorrow?
That is tomorrow morning
Now the crickets are singing, aren't they?
And the bugle is sounding the last post, isn't it?
Trains are still running
It's not the witching hour yet, is it?

THE END

Slaughterhouse

In the slaughterhouse,
the cow, about to die, mooed!
The June field's earth was red,
on the horizon clouds were floating.

     The road is bad enough to trip you;
     at that time I was sick.

In the slaughterhouse,
the cow, about to die, mooed!
The June field's earth was red,
on the horizon clouds were floating.

Desert

In the desert
  I saw fire!
In the desert
  I saw fire!
   That,
     what was it?
   That,
     what was it?
Heatwaves, above the rippled sand,
  are trembling.
Heatwaves, above the rippled sand,
  are trembling.
   In the desert sky
    I saw fire!
   In the desert sky
    I saw fire!
That,
   what was it?
That,
   what was it?
    Tired camel,
      taciturn Turk.[1]
That,
   what was it?
    Tired camel
      sees its own shadow.
    Taciturn Turk
      glares enviously.
Beyond the dunes,
  I saw fire.
Beyond the dunes,
  I saw fire.

Mountain Stream

The beer cooled in the mountain stream
was sad like youth.
Looking up at the summit, I
drank as if incessantly weeping.

Soaking wet and almost coming off, the label too
was sad like youth.
But everyone just said, "It's really good".
I actually said so too.

The damp moss and the foaming water
and the shade and the rocks were sad.
By and by everyone stopped knocking it back.
The beer was still cooling in the mountain stream.

Looking through the water at the bottle glass,
I felt that I no longer wanted to walk.
I excused myself, went to an inn,
and talked to the maid.

Notes

3) [1]Rice crackers – *senbei* – are golden when toasted and come in many shapes, including discs. Nakahara is perhaps comparing the setting sun, occluded by a zinc roof, to such a cracker.

5) [1]'Yu-an, yu-yon': the transliteration reproduces the sound value of this meaningless line, which may have been intended to evoke the swinging of the trapeze artist.

6) [1]'beauty spot': exactly that – a stick-on beauty patch like those fashionable in 18th-century Europe.

13) [1]'rootcrop': *daikon*, known to English-speakers as *mooli*, the large carrotlike white radish used in Japanese cooking. Nakahara evokes only the plant's green head, protruding from the ground.
    [2]'aé ao': a meaningless sound effect.
    [3]'my mother's neatly tied sash': *obijime*, a thick braided cord in bright and contrasting colours, wound round the outside of the *obi* and tied to keep it in place.

14) [1]'under the floor': the gap between the earth and the floor was, and is, a feature of most Japanese dwellings. It allows air to circulate during the hot summer months and prevents damp rising into the fabric.

17) [1]'long pipes': *kiseru*; familiar from *ukiyo-e* prints of courtesans, these are rod-shaped pipes with a tiny metal bowl at the far end holding enough tobacco for a few puffs.
    [2]'dressing gowns': *dotera*, a heavy quilted jacket, informal apparel generally worn indoors.
    [3]'I lost a chair': the end of the poem could perhaps have been intended to mean 'I lost my place in life'. But the ostensible meaning of the Japanese is as given here.

116

18) [1]Kawakami Tetsutarō (1902–80): Nakahara's close friend and later a prominent literary, cultural and music critic who wrote at length about his work (see Introduction).

27) [1]'Michiko': Ōoka Shōhei has written that the original Michiko was Hayama Michiko, the screen name of Ishikawa Seiko, another film actress who lodged in Kyoto at the same lodgings as Yasuko. Nakahara later described her to Ōoka as an ideal woman. The 'ideal woman' was also sister-in-law to Tanizaki Junichirō, and when Nakahara knew her she had already lived for some years in a *ménage à trois* with her sister Chiyo and Tanizaki, who apparently preferred her as partner in his favourite masochistic sex games. Tanizaki scripted some of her film roles, and she supposedly was his model for the go-getting Naomi, a teenage bar hostess with a face like Mary Pickford's, who is the central character of his 1924 novel *Chijin no ai* (translated as *Naomi*).

29) [1]Abe Rokurō (1904–57): Nakahara's close friend; teacher, critic and one of the coterie *Hakuchigun* (see Introduction).
   [2]'clumsy gardeners': by implication, Nakahara's parents, whom the poet blames for his botched upbringing.

30) [1]The original Japanese makes it clear that the first voice in Part 2 of the poem is a man; while the second, and the narrator of Part 3, is a woman.

31) [1]'*tōfu* vendors' horns': itinerant *tōfu* sellers were common sights in Taishō and early Shōwa Japan, pulling their handcarts full of fresh *tōfu* round their beats morning and evening, announcing their arrival by blowing their horns. Fresh *tōfu* decays quickly, especially in the heat of summer, hence the need for frequent deliveries.
   [2]'fifteen stone': 30 *kan* (an old unit; 1 *kan* = 3.75 kg).

32) [1]Sekiguchi Takakatsu: a university friend of Kobayashi Hideo who lived with Nakahara for a while.

34) [1]Kitahara Hakushū (1885–1942): a notable poet from the generation before Nakahara. The poem quoted, from his 1911 collection *Omoide* (Memories), is in the old *imayō* form: four lines of seven plus five syllables.

38) [1] Yasuhara Yoshihiro (b. 1908): Nakahara's best friend during his Tokyo years. He later published a collection of Nakahara's letters to him.

39) [1] 'at the table': the writer is actually seated at the *kotatsu*, the traditional low table with a brazier or other heat source underneath it and a quilted skirt of blanket material fastened round its rim and extending outwards on all sides. In cold weather, those seated round the *kotatsu* can warm their legs and arms under the blanket.

49) [1] 'an empty cigarette packet': an empty carton of Golden Bat, the most popular brand in pre-war Japan, though now less favoured. The bat was originally a Chinese symbol for good fortune (homophonous with 'bat' in Chinese); two bats were depicted on the label along with the brand name in English.

57) [1] 'sprites': 'kobolds' in the original, but the Japanese usage of this imported term denotes an airier being than the German original.

59) [1] 'pattens': *bokuri*, a variety of *geta*, the wooden thonged sandals worn by all classes in feudal Japan and still seen today.

62) [1] 'Void Autumn'; originally a cycle of some twenty poems, of which this is the only one to have survived, as it was set to music by Moroi Saburō (see Introduction). According to Sekiguchi, Nakahara composed the entire cycle overnight, but lost the manuscript of the other poems while he was drunk.

66) [1] Shinjuku: though bustling and growing, the Shinjuku of the Taishō and early Shōwa eras was not the dynamic nexus it is in today's Tokyo. The district was only incorporated (partially) within the city limits in 1920, and looking towards Shinjuku would, in Nakahara's time, still have given the sensation of looking out of the city into the distance.

67) [1] 'boiled greens': *mitsuba*, a trefoil normally used as a garnish. Nakahara reportedly loved the dish: Sekiguchi spoke of his eating it every day.

81) [1] 'New Year's Bell': *Joya-no-kane*, the temple bell rung 108 times at midnight on New Year's Eve to ring away the sins of the old year. New Year is Japan's most important holiday, with traditional associations much like Christmas in the West.

[2]'*soba*': buckwheat noodles, eaten for good luck on New Year's Eve, so that one's luck may go on as long as the long *soba*.

[3]'Ginza and Asakusa': at their peak in the inter-war years as Tokyo's centres for, respectively, high-life and low-life fun. The crowds are out for *hatsumōde*, the lucky first visit of the New Year to Buddhist temples or Shinto shrines.

86) [1]See Introduction for Nakahara's early sojourn in Kyoto.

91) [1]'I tucked it into my sleeve': at this time *kimono* were still common wear. Carrying small items in *kimono* sleeves was a usual practice, as everyday as putting something in a pocket.

92) [1]The poem was written after the death of Nakahara's first son, Fumiya, in November 1936.

93) [1]'Tircis and Aminte': lady minstrels, characters taken from *Mandoline*, one of Paul Verlaine's *Fêtes Galantes*.

96) [1]'Chōmon Gorge': Chōmon-kyō, a gorge in Yamaguchi Prefecture.

97) [1]Marunouchi Building: finished in 1923, this office building was the largest structure in Taishō Japan. It survived the 1923 earthquake and the wartime firestorms; today it is dwarfed by the other, larger Marunouchi Buildings which followed it.

105) [1]This poem is a continuation of 'Self-Portrait on a Cold Night', but was published separately at a later date.

107) [1]'Dry Riverbed': *Mizunashi-gawara* in Yamaguchi Prefecture. Nakahara's family originated in this area, and the family grave, where Nakahara himself would one day be buried, is in a graveyard near the riverbed. The figure whose grave is mentioned is Nakahara's brother Kōzō, who died in 1931.

114) [1]'Turk' is written with the Chinese characters traditionally used for that nationality, but Nakahara gave them the phonetic gloss 'Dutch'. The name therefore reads simultaneously as 'Turk' and 'Dutchman'. Whether Nakahara meant anything by this, whether he intended 'Dutch' to have another meaning, or whether he simply put the wrong sound values for the characters are all questions still debated by critics.

Bibliography

The text used for the translation was *Nakahara Chūya*
(Nihon shijin zenshū #22), Shinchōsha, Tokyo, 1967; with
occasional reference made to *Nakahara Chūya shishū:*
Yogorechimatta kanashimi ni, Shūeisha, Tokyo, 1991.

References consulted
Aoki Ken, *Uchinaru Nakahara Chūya*, Mugi Shobō, Tokyo,
   1975
Fukakusa Shishirō, *Waga rinjin Nakahara Chūya*, Mugi
   Shobō, Tokyo, 1974
Fundō Junsaku, *Nakahara Chūya*, Kōdansha, Tokyo, 1974
Katō Shūichi, *A History of Japanese Literature: Volume 3,*
   The Modern Years, (English translation) Macmillan,
   London, 1983
Keene, Donald, *Dawn to the West: Volume 2, Poetry, Drama*
   and Criticism, Holt, Rhinehart and Wilson, New York,
   1984
Murakami Mamoru, *Nakahara Chūya no shi to shogai*,
   Daiichi Shuppan, Tokyo, 1979
Ōoka Shōhei, *Nakahara Chuya*, Kōdansha, Tokyo, 1989
Ōoka Shōhei and Sato Yasumasa, *Nakahara Chūya no shi no*
   sekai, Kyōbunkan, Tokyo, 1985
Thunman, Noriko, *Nakahara Chūya and French Symbolism*,
   University of Stockholm, 1983

Index of Titles

121

CPSIA information can be obtained
at www.ICGtesting.com
Printed in the USA
BVHW072115230322
632274BV00004B/114